Contents

Who Is
Richard Branson?

Who Is
Richard Branson?

by Michael Burgan

illustrated by Ted Hammond

ıse

To Debbie, for all her support and love—MB

To my mom—TH

PENGUIN WORKSHOP
Penguin Young Readers Group
An Imprint of Penguin Random House LLC

Text copyright © 2015 by Michael Burgan. Illustrations copyright © 2015 by Penguin Random House LLC. All rights reserved. Published by Penguin Workshop, an imprint of Penguin Random House LLC, 345 Hudson Street, New York, New York 10014. PENGUIN and PENGUIN WORKSHOP are trademarks of Penguin Books Ltd. WHO HQ & Design is a registered trademark of Penguin Random House LLC. Printed in the USA.

Library of Congress Control Number: 2015947743

ISBN 9780448483153   10 9 8 7 6 5 4

Who Is
Richard Branson?

During the 1950s, the Branson family took a vacation to the beach in Devon, England. On the trip, five-year-old Ricky's aunt Joyce made a bet with him. She would pay him if he could learn to swim before the end of their vacation.

Ricky spent the whole vacation trying to teach himself how to swim. Most of the time, he kept one foot on the sandy sea bottom and hopped along in the water. Waves would roll over him as he fought to keep the cold water out of his mouth. By the last day of the vacation, Ricky had not learned how to swim. Aunt Joyce told him he could try again next year. But Ricky wasn't ready to give up. He wanted to win the bet.

Ricky made one last try to learn how to swim. His family gathered around to watch. Ricky saw his mother smile, as if she were thinking, "You can do it!" He took a deep breath, went into the water, and then moved his arms and legs as best he could. He was swimming! Going around in a circle, he heard his family cheering. When Ricky came ashore, Aunt Joyce handed him the money for winning the bet. Ricky later said that even though it was only about two dollars, it "seemed like a fortune."

As Ricky Branson grew up, he built a real fortune. He started many companies. Some of his businesses failed, but several became very successful. The world came to know him as the billionaire Richard Branson. And just as when he was a boy, he took plenty of risks. He learned to sail boats and to fly hot-air balloons. He even bought a rocket that could take him into space. Richard lived by this thought: "If you've got a great idea, you need to just give it a try. And if you fall flat on your face, pick yourself up and try again."

Chapter 1
Early Challenges

On July 18, 1950, Richard Branson was born in London, England. Times were tough for his parents, Eve and Ted Branson. Ted was struggling to start his career as a lawyer, and the couple had little money. Eve helped out by making furniture cushions and selling them in the local shops. The family had just bought a small cottage in the countryside of Surrey.

His parents called their newborn son Ricky, though later everyone came to call him Richard. The Bransons didn't have a car. Ted drove the family's motorcycle while Eve sat behind him.

She held on tight to Ricky's baby carriage, which bounced along behind the bike. Baby Ricky seemed to enjoy the adventure, watching the scenery passing by.

Over the next few years, Eve Branson expanded
her little business of selling cushions. She began
to make wooden boxes and wastebaskets that she
sold at Harrods, a large London department store.
Ricky watched her work in a shed behind the
family cottage. Eve was always trying to build her
business.

Still, it wasn't all work and no play for the Bransons. Eve and Ted enjoyed spending time with Ricky and the two sisters who followed him, Lindy and Vanessa. They were always a close family. As the Bransons earned more money, they were able to afford a van. The family would head off with the children sprawled out on a mattress in the back of the van. The Bransons talked about many things,

from Ted's legal cases to current events in the news. Ricky's parents wanted him and his sisters to think for themselves. They encouraged their children to freely express their own opinions.

Eve Branson also wanted her children to be comfortable in front of people. So when the Bransons had company, Ricky had to sing for the guests. He was sometimes shy around strangers, and he didn't like performing. Little by little, though, he got used to it. And he learned that he enjoyed entertaining people.

Ricky was a playful, energetic boy. He loved to climb trees and ride his bike. He also worked in the family garden and helped his mother around the house. Ricky was great at sports. He ran races and played soccer and rugby. School, though, was a challenge. In the classroom, he struggled to read the blackboard until he got glasses at around age ten. He also had a condition called dyslexia that made it difficult for him to learn.

With dyslexia a person may not see numbers
and letters in the correct order. They often have
trouble reading, switching one letter for another.
They might write "mawn lower" instead of "lawn
mower."

At eight, Ricky left home to go to Scaitcliffe, a boarding school in Surrey. Ted Branson had gone to boarding schools, too, as did most British boys whose families could afford it. They helped boys learn how to live away from their families and become independent.

Because of his dyslexia, Ricky struggled with schoolwork. Scaitcliffe allowed teachers to spank students with a cane if they made mistakes.

Ricky was punished this way about once a week for simple mistakes such as giving the wrong date of a historic event. The beatings didn't help Ricky improve in school. His grades remained poor, and his parents were afraid he would not be able to get into a good high school. After about three years, the Bransons sent Ricky to a new school, Cliff View House.

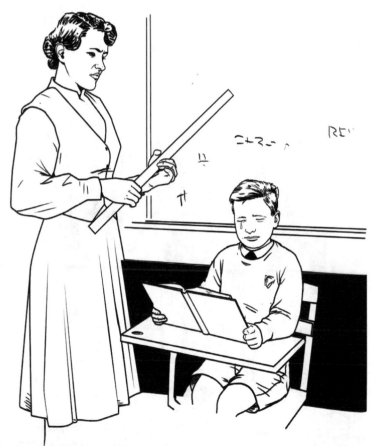

Cliff View House was a special school for students who struggled to learn. Students studied constantly. For Ricky, that meant going a whole year without playing sports. But at his new school, Ricky worked hard and his grades improved.

In September 1964, Ricky entered Stowe, a boarding school in Buckinghamshire. At Stowe, younger students like fourteen-year-old Ricky had to act as servants for the older boys. They had to run errands for them or do their chores.

Stowe also forced all the boys to watch the school's sporting events. Ricky would have preferred to have the time for himself. He disliked most of the rules, and school was still a challenge for him.

But Ricky developed a new interest at Stowe. He had seen his mother earn money by working from home. He wanted to start his own business, too. He and his friend Nik Powell decided to grow and sell Christmas trees. The Bransons had just bought a new, bigger home in Surrey with plenty of land. The two teens had lots of space for their new business. Within a year, Ricky figured, the trees would be big enough to sell at Christmastime.

The idea might have worked—if rabbits hadn't eaten all the young trees.

Despite the failure, Ricky had learned something about himself. When he tried to do math in school, his dyslexia made it very difficult to come up with the right answer. But in planning his Christmas tree business, he also had to do math. He needed to figure out the total cost of the trees and how many he would need to sell to make a profit. Suddenly, the numbers made more sense, and he actually *enjoyed* doing the math!

At Stowe, Ricky also began to improve his writing. He even won a writing contest. Ricky became so confident with his writing that he and his friend Jonny Holland-Gems decided to start a magazine. Ricky's parents had raised him to be independent and think for himself. He later said, "I have always thought rules were there to be broken." So in their magazine, he and Jonny wanted to write about all of the Stowe rules they thought were so unfair. But they didn't want to publish it just for Stowe students. They wanted other teenagers to read it, too. They called the magazine *Student*.

Barely fifteen, Ricky called his parents and said he wanted to leave school to publish his magazine. Eve and Ted Branson made a deal with Ricky: He could drop out of school, but first he had to pass at least one class. Ricky dropped all his other classes to focus on only one subject: ancient history.

Then, he spent hours creating the first issue of *Student*. He wrote letters to famous people seeking interviews. He called companies asking them to buy advertisements. He was so young he never stopped to think how crazy it might be to try to start a magazine.

By 1967, Ricky had passed his ancient history class. His parents kept their part of the agreement and let Ricky leave Stowe. He and Jonny planned to move to London and focus all their attention on *Student* magazine. As Ricky said good-bye to the man who ran the school, the headmaster's parting words to him were, "I predict that you will either go to prison or become a millionaire." He knew that Richard Branson was determined to succeed. But he wasn't sure where Richard's love of breaking the rules would lead him.

Chapter 2
First Businesses

Just seventeen, Richard Branson left the countryside and moved to one of the most exciting cities in the world. Great Britain had struggled to rebuild after the destruction it suffered during World War II.

But now many people had better jobs and the economy was improving. The capital was nicknamed "Swinging London." By 1967 the city had become a center for fashion, music, and art. Much of the new music was popular with teens around Richard's age. He wanted to write about music and other things the young people of London were interested in.

But starting *Student* wasn't easy. Richard and Jonny Gems moved into the basement of the Gemses' home. They had no money, and they slept on mattresses tossed on the basement floor. Eve Branson sometimes came down from Surrey to bring them food.

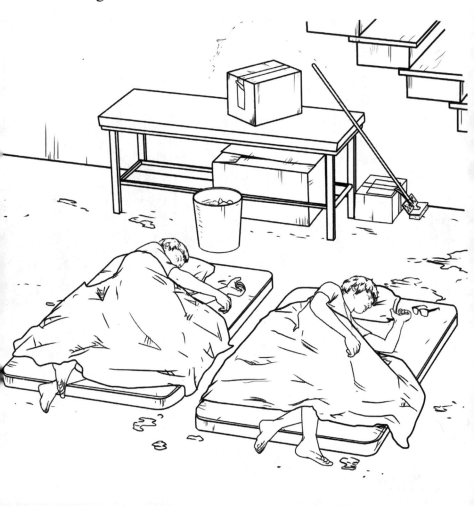

They set up their office in a dusty crypt—an underground vault sometimes used as a tomb— under a church. A local minister had loaned them the space for free. Richard and Jonny worked so hard, they didn't even seem to notice the coffins all around them. Richard put a slab of rock on top of two of the coffins and used it as a desk!

Jonny knew which musicians were popular and what world events teenagers were talking about. He came up with most of the ideas for the magazine's articles. Meanwhile, Richard managed the business side of *Student*. He kept looking for companies to buy ads, and contacted entertainers and government leaders for interviews. Richard was charming and had a way of convincing people to work with him. He was also stubborn. He refused to give up if people first said "no."

The first issue of *Student* appeared in January 1968. The two most important British bands of the time were the Rolling Stones and the Beatles.

THE ROLLING STONES

Richard and Jonny enjoyed blasting both bands' music while they worked. Richard turned on the charm and convinced Mick Jagger, the lead singer of the Rolling Stones, to be interviewed for *Student*.

THE BEATLES

And Richard and Jonny both met with guitarist and singer John Lennon of the Beatles. Both Jagger and Lennon were immensely popular. Richard hoped these two major interviews would convince young people to buy *Student*. Having world-famous rock stars in the magazine made the more established British newspapers, magazines, and radio stations take *Student* seriously—even if its publishers were still in their teens.

Richard also wanted to write about the Vietnam War. Young people around the world thought that US involvement in Vietnam was a mistake. They felt that Vietnam was in the middle of a civil war and the United States had no right to interfere.

Richard and the *Student* staff protested against the war in Vietnam. A German television station asked Richard to speak about his opinions on the politics of the war. Soon, people across Great Britain learned more about Richard Branson as newspapers began to write about him *and* his magazine.

THE VIETNAM WAR

SHORTLY AFTER VIETNAM WON ITS INDEPENDENCE FROM FRANCE IN 1954, THE COUNTRY WAS DIVIDED IN TWO. IN THE NORTH, VIETNAMESE COMMUNISTS CONTROLLED THE GOVERNMENT. THEY BELIEVED THAT THE GOVERNMENT SHOULD HAVE CONTROL OVER MOST OF THE BUSINESSES AND OWN MOST OF THE LAND. THEY DENIED THE PEOPLE LIVING THERE THE RIGHT TO FREE SPEECH. ONLY MEMBERS OF THE COMMUNIST PARTY COULD BE ELECTED TO OFFICE.

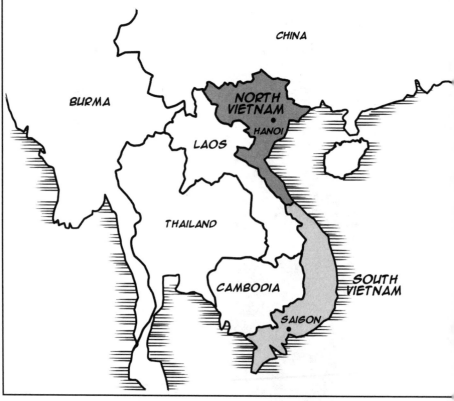

THE UNITED STATES SUPPORTED THE GOVERNMENT OF SOUTH VIETNAM, AS ITS LEADERS OPPOSED COMMUNISM. MAJOR FIGHTING IN THE WAR BETWEEN THE NORTH AND SOUTH BEGAN IN 1959. AFTER THAT, THE US SENT MONEY, SUPPLIES, AND SOLDIERS TO HELP THE SOUTH VIETNAMESE IN THEIR FIGHT AGAINST THE COMMUNISTS. BY 1969, MORE THAN FIVE HUNDRED THOUSAND US TROOPS WERE IN VIETNAM. BY THE WAR'S END MORE THAN FIFTY-EIGHT THOUSAND AMERICANS HAD DIED. THE NUMBER WAS MUCH HIGHER FOR THE VIETNAMESE POPULATION. AROUND THE WORLD, PEOPLE PROTESTED AGAINST THE UNITED STATES' INVOLVEMENT.

MOST US TROOPS FINALLY LEFT VIETNAM IN 1973. TWO YEARS LATER, NORTH VIETNAM WON THE WAR AND UNITED THE COUNTRY UNDER COMMUNIST RULE.

Young people were speaking up and hoping to make changes in society and government. Richard and *Student* were giving a voice to that movement.

Late in 1968, Jonny Gems decided to go back to school. Richard struggled to run *Student* on his own. He asked his old friend Nik Powell to help. Together they kept *Student* going for two more years.

At first, no one who worked on the magazine was paid. *Student* wasn't making any money. Richard and his friends relied on the food, and sometimes money, that Eve Branson gave them.

Over time, Richard finally made a little money and paid the staff, though he couldn't afford much. Richard was still not making enough money at *Student* to support himself.

But Richard kept the staff happy with the parties he threw at a house his parents rented for him. Everyone pitched in whatever they could. Richard liked to have fun and he wanted everyone who worked on the magazine to have fun, too.

But working at *Student* meant more than just having fun. Richard made it clear to everyone that the magazine was doing something useful. It was providing young people with information about the world around them.

In 1970 Richard finally found a way to earn his living. He knew how much his staff and all  the young people he knew enjoyed rock music. Most music was sold on seven- and twelve-inch-wide records made of vinyl. People bought them at record shops or large department stores. Richard thought he could make money selling records another way—by mail. Customers would send in an order form and the payment for the records they wanted. He would buy the records and mail them to the customers. Richard promised he could find any record a customer requested. He called his new business Virgin Mail Order.

At first, Richard bought records from a London business that charged him a low price because he bought such a large quantity. Later, he bought directly from record companies. With both methods, Richard was able to offer lower prices than the record stores. He didn't have to pay rent on a store or hire a lot of employees. His customers got the music they wanted at lower prices than in the stores, and Richard still made a profit.

Virgin Mail Order quickly had many new customers. But Richard ran into trouble in 1971 when postal workers in England went on strike. They refused to work until they were paid more money. The strike was bad news for Virgin. How would it send records to its customers? Richard decided it would be a good idea to have his own record store in addition to his mail-order business. But he wanted it to be unlike the other record stores in London.

Richard created a store that welcomed teenagers.

The staff was young and eager to talk about new
music. Customers could listen to music on
headphones before they bought it. Richard also
made sure the store carried records that customers
couldn't easily find anywhere else. Many of these
records came from other European countries or the
United States. His young customers appreciated
the effort Richard made for them. They felt that

Richard cared about them because he was one of them. Kids, teenagers, and young adults flocked to Virgin Records.

Running his record business, however, was not always easy. The expenses of running Virgin Mail Order grew, and sometimes customers claimed they never received a certain record when they actually had. Richard had to take their word and send another record. That meant he lost money.

In 1970, Richard bought a mansion in a village called Shipton-on-Cherwell. The large home had been built in the seventeenth century and had acres of woods surrounding it. Richard called it the Manor. He wanted to turn it into a recording

studio where bands could live while they recorded their music. But it was an expensive idea. To buy the Manor, Richard had to borrow money from a bank and from his family. His debts soared.

To save money, Richard did not pay the British government taxes on several orders of records.
He wanted to use the tax money to pay his debts.
Richard knew this wasn't the right thing to do.
But he told himself he would start paying the taxes after he paid back the money he owed the bank.

Before that could happen, Richard was caught and arrested. He was ashamed, but later he called the arrest "one of the best things that has ever happened to me."

In school, he had always enjoyed breaking or challenging the rules. But now he saw that in business, he could not break the law. He came to an agreement with the British government. He would pay all the taxes plus a fine. With the help of his family, he paid the government what he owed. And he promised himself he would never break the law again.

Then Richard took the first steps toward making the Virgin name famous around the world.

Chapter 3
A Growing Company

Throughout 1971 and 1972, Virgin Records opened more stores. Richard hired his cousin Simon Draper to choose which records to sell. Richard said that Simon "knew more about music than anyone I'd ever met." This was one of Richard's great skills in business. He came up with good ideas and then found the right people to help him make them happen.

Rock bands were now recording at the Manor.

One day while visiting the studio, Richard met a nineteen-year-old American woman named Kristen Tomassi. Kristen knew a musician who was recording at the Manor, and he had invited her to come along. Richard immediately liked Kristen and soon they began dating. They married a little more than a year later, in July 1972.

The Manor was becoming even more important for Richard's business. With Simon's help, Richard started his own record company. Bands signed contracts with companies like his, and the companies sold their records. At the time, the major record companies included EMI in Great Britain and Atlantic Records in the United States. In 1973, Richard released the first four albums by his new Virgin Records. One was called *Tubular Bells*, by Mike Oldfield. It became a huge hit.

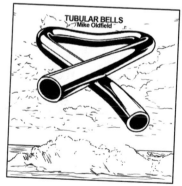

The record was unlike most music of the day. Oldfield combined rock music with other styles, such as classical music and folk music. Sales of the record increased dramatically after parts of *Tubular Bells* were used in the popular horror movie *The Exorcist*. It was at this time, Richard said, "the money started rolling in."

As Richard made more money, he did not change his lifestyle very much. He was in his early twenties. He wanted to feel relaxed and have fun whenever he could. He went to meetings wearing sweaters, instead of a jacket and tie like most businessmen wore. At parties, he liked to surprise people by dressing up in women's clothing. And he loved to play practical jokes.

Richard liked to live simply. Although he
owned a nice home in London, he loved to spend
time on a houseboat he owned on a canal in the
city. Richard sometimes worked from the boat,
staying in touch with the Virgin staff by phone.

By 1974, Virgin Records was doing well. But Richard and Kristen were having trouble in their marriage. Although they tried to keep their marriage together, they divorced in 1976.

By then, Virgin was trying to sign hugely

popular bands such as The Who and the Rolling Stones. This was difficult because bigger record labels offered bands more money than Virgin could pay. So Richard pushed to find undiscovered bands and new ways to expand the Virgin brand. He created Virgin Rags to sell clothing. He bought a restaurant. He started a sandwich delivery service.

In all his businesses, Richard tried to give customers a good product at the lowest price. Richard didn't always stop to consider if the new businesses could make money. He seemed thrilled to simply form new companies and give customers what they wanted.

In 1977, Virgin Records signed a new group called the Sex Pistols. They were one of Britain's first punk rock bands. Their songs made fun of the Queen of England and British society.

SEX PISTOLS

The band brought Virgin Records major attention and publicity, which Richard enjoyed. He hoped other bands would now want to record with Virgin Records, too.

Things were also looking better for Richard in his personal life. He had met Joan Templeman in 1976, but they did not start dating until two years later. On one of their first vacations, they went to the British Virgin Islands in the Caribbean Sea. They visited a small island that was for sale. It was called Necker Island. To Richard and Joan, this spot was like paradise. Richard decided to buy it.

NECKER ISLAND

BRITISH VIRGIN ISLANDS

JOST VAN DYKE

VIRGIN GORDA

TORTOLA

ST. THOMAS

ST. JOHN

ST. CROIX

US VIRGIN ISLANDS

Now more than ever, he wanted his Virgin companies to succeed so he and Joan could build a home on their beautiful island.

In 1979, Joan became pregnant, but the baby was born too early and did not live. The loss was hard on both her and Richard, but they decided to try to have another child. Holly Branson was born in 1981.

BRITISH PUNK MUSIC

THE SEX PISTOLS WERE ONE OF THE MOST FAMOUS PUNK BANDS OF THE 1970S. PUNK ROCK, WITH ITS SIMPLE RHYTHMS AND STEADY BEAT, WAS ALL ABOUT YOUTHFUL REBELLION AND ANGER. BRITAIN WAS NOW FACING TOUGH TIMES. MANY PEOPLE WERE OUT OF WORK. THE SEX PISTOLS SANG THAT BRITISH YOUTH HAD "NO FUTURE."

OTHER POPULAR BRITISH PUNK BANDS INCLUDED THE CLASH AND SIOUXSIE AND THE BANSHEES. SOME PUNK MUSICIANS WERE DIRECTLY INFLUENCED BY THE SHORT, FAST, AND LOUD SONGS THAT WERE PLAYED BY SUCH US BANDS AS THE NEW YORK DOLLS AND THE RAMONES.

MANY PUNK MUSICIANS COULD NOT PLAY THEIR INSTRUMENTS WELL. THE GROUPS AND THEIR FANS OFTEN WORE RIPPED CLOTHES, LEATHER JACKETS, SAFETY PINS, AND CHAINS. WITH BOTH THEIR MUSIC AND THEIR PERSONAL STYLE, PUNKS WANTED TO SHOCK THE ESTABLISHED, ADULT WORLD.

Virgin Records was going strong. The company was now selling more than just records. It had opened its first Megastore, offering records, books, video games, movies, and more. *Mega*—which refers to something that is very large—perfectly described the way that Richard thought about his booming business. And, as always, he was thinking about new opportunities to explore.

Chapter 4
Virgin Takes to the Skies

Richard was driven to put the Virgin name on even more companies. He believed having many different businesses made sense. When one company was going through a bad time, another would most likely be doing well. In this way, Virgin would never lose a lot of money at once. But being interested in new things was also a part of Richard's personality. He liked to explore new ideas and take on new challenges. The thought of doing the same thing over and over bored him.

With their increasing wealth, Richard and Joan bought a cottage close to the Manor recording studio. They also bought a new home in London, and in 1984, they completed their dream home on Necker Island in the Caribbean.

Richard cherished the island as a place where friends and family could come to relax.

That same year, Richard took on his biggest challenge ever. In February 1984, an American lawyer named Randolph Fields tempted Richard with a new idea. Fields wanted him to help pay for a new airline that would fly between London and the United States. Richard wasn't really sure about Fields's idea. Airlines need large amounts of money to buy planes and fuel. And Great Britain already had British Airways, a large company that offered many flights around the world. But as Richard later wrote, "The idea of operating a Virgin airline grabbed my attention."

Within a few days, Richard decided to take the risk. He thought he could make money by repeating what he had done with his record business. He would offer customers low prices and give better service. Richard called Simon Draper to discuss the idea.

"You're crazy," his cousin said.

"I'm serious," Richard replied.

Richard had already done some research. He could rent a plane from the airplane-maker Boeing for one year. If the new airline wasn't profitable,

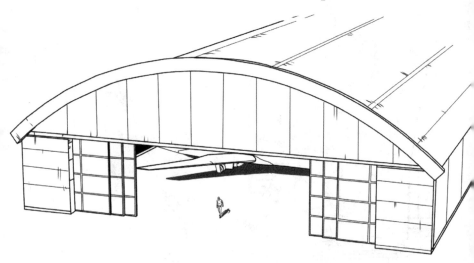

Virgin could simply close the business after the first year. He argued with Simon and others in the company that Virgin could afford to give the airline business a try. More money was flowing in thanks to the international success of new artists, like Phil Collins and Culture Club, on the Virgin Records label. Besides, he told his colleagues, "It'll be fun."

Despite the questions Simon and the others raised, Richard charged ahead.

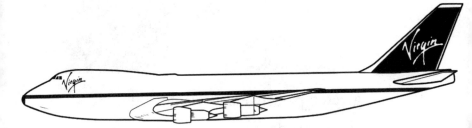

Just a few months later, in June 1984, Virgin Atlantic Airways was ready for its first flight.

Richard greeted passengers wearing a pilot's
uniform. Joan, his daughter Holly, and some
friends were on board, along with reporters and
entertainers. Richard turned the flight into a
party, playing music over the loudspeakers and
offering everyone drinks and chocolate ice cream.

Although the first flight went smoothly,
Richard still knew that running an airline would
not be easy. But he was determined to make
Virgin Atlantic just as successful as his record
company.

Chapter 5
Breaking World Records

Richard was always on the lookout for new ways to promote Virgin Atlantic Airways. He tried several times to break the speed record for crossing the Atlantic Ocean on boats named *Virgin Atlantic Challenger* and *Virgin Atlantic Challenger II*.

Richard sailed on both boats, crossing the Atlantic in just over three days. While onboard the first *Challenger* in August 1985, his mother radioed him with some good news: Joan had just had a baby boy. Back on land, someone showed Richard a picture of the baby that had appeared in a local newspaper, and he felt overwhelmed with joy. He and Joan named their son Sam.

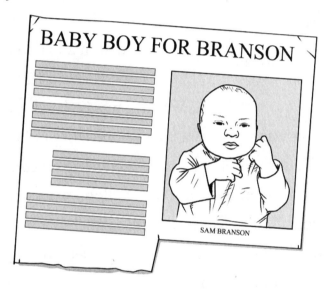

BABY BOY FOR BRANSON

SAM BRANSON

In 1987, Richard made plans to cross the Atlantic again—in a balloon! Richard quickly learned how to fly balloons, and he fell in love with the views from several thousand feet in the air.

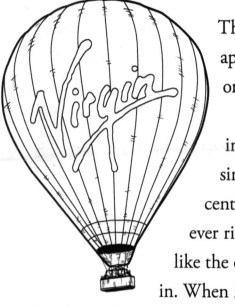

The Virgin name appeared in huge letters on his hot-air balloon. People have flown in hot-air balloons since the eighteenth century. But no one had ever ridden in a balloon like the one Richard flew in. When it was inflated, the balloon was as tall as a twenty-one-story building.

The success of the Atlantic crossing relied on several new innovations. The balloon would fly at about 27,000 feet in the air—much higher than others had in the past. Strong jet-stream winds would push it along at fast speeds—up to 140 miles per hour. Richard and his partner Per Lindstrand rode in a special cabin that provided air, radios, and navigation equipment to help them guide the balloon in flight.

On July 2, Richard and Lindstrand lifted
off from Maine. The balloon was soon soaring
across the ocean at record speeds. The next day,

the balloonists spotted Ireland. They flew close to the ground to cast off extra fuel tanks, and briefly touched land. Then the balloon soared skyward again. Lindstrand had trouble controlling the craft, and soon it was flying low over the ocean. The cabin holding the men hit the water. A mechanical problem prevented them from releasing the balloon as they had planned. Richard and Lindstrand prepared to jump out into the water. Only Lindstrand made it. After he jumped, the balloon shot up again. Richard was alone. And he felt certain he was going to die.

Richard had to act fast. He cut off the fuel to the balloon so it would sink. Then he climbed out of the cabin and prepared to jump into the water. A rescue helicopter was already flying nearby. Richard jumped into the cold water. The life jacket he wore quickly brought him to the surface. He said, "It was heaven. I was alive."

The helicopter picked him up and then found
Per Lindstrand. The two men hugged each other,
glad that they had survived. And they had also
made history. Richard and Lindstrand were
the first people to cross the Atlantic in a hot-
air balloon! Afterward, Richard hinted that his
adventurous ways were over.

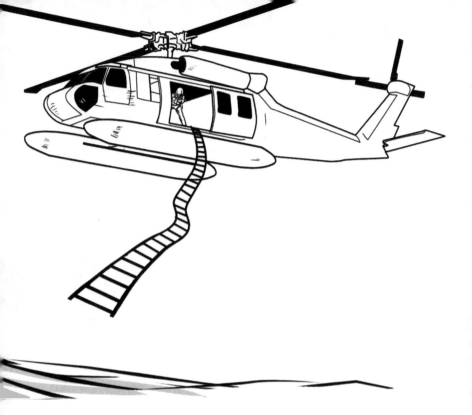

But his love of ballooning led to even more
trips and more records. In January 1991, he and
Lindstrand crossed the Pacific Ocean in a hot-air
balloon. They were the first people to do so. The
two men were in the air for just over forty-six
hours—another world record! Later, they made
three different attempts to fly around the world.

They failed, but along the way, Virgin built the
largest fleet of hot-air balloons in Great
Britain. And Richard showed the world
that a successful businessman could also
have a daring, adventurous side.

Chapter 6
Billionaire

Richard Branson's exciting adventures brought him and his company more attention than ever before. But away from the balloons and the boats, he worked hard to keep his businesses growing.

In 1985, Richard combined his many different companies into a larger one called The Virgin Group. Virgin Atlantic Airways remained a major focus. By the end of 1989, in addition to its flights to New York, the airline had added two more routes to cities in the United States. It also had a route to Japan. Richard took a personal interest

in Virgin's customers and employees. At times, he would fly on his own airline and ask passengers what the company could do better.

That same year, he and Joan married on Necker Island. Holly and Sam were part of the ceremony.

Richard—as usual—arrived in a very unexpected way. Guests looked up to see a helicopter slowly coming down—with Richard hanging from its bottom landing skids! Joan came to accept the fact that Richard would always love attention-getting stunts.

Richard was becoming known as "the smiley man with the beard." *Smiling is good for business*, he thought. A smile could ease tensions in a business meeting or convince people he cared about their interests. No matter what happened in his personal or private life, Richard believed in the value of the smile.

At the time, the largest airline in Great Britain was British Airways (BA). It was not happy to see

Virgin taking away its passengers and gaining more routes. Richard became convinced that BA was out to destroy Virgin Atlantic. And he was right.

BA began to gather information about Virgin. It used the information to offer cheaper flights to passengers. The company later denied that it had done anything wrong. It also said Richard was only seeking more public attention. Richard sued BA for lying about him. In 1993, Richard won his court case against BA. The case boosted Richard's

popularity in Great Britain. People liked the idea that a man who started his own business as a teenager had challenged a much bigger company and won. Richard saw himself as the small businessman taking on the corporate giant.

Before Richard won his case, Virgin Records finally signed the Rolling Stones in November 1991. Almost twenty-five years had passed since Richard played their music in the offices of *Student*.

Yet the Stones remained one of the most famous rock bands in the world. Signing them had cost at least $44 million. This only added to Virgin Records' already large debt.

Richard realized there was only one way to pay all his debts. He had to sell Virgin Records. Joan and some of Richard's friends told him not to do it. They thought he would regret selling his first hugely successful company. But in 1992, when another record company offered Richard $1 billion for Virgin Records, he couldn't refuse. The money paid off Virgin's debts and some of Richard's business partners. What Richard kept helped make him worth more than $1 billion.

With the money he made from selling Virgin Records, Richard looked for new opportunities. The Virgin Group started the first national commercial radio station in Great Britain. It created its own brand of cola, to compete with Coke and Pepsi.

And in 1997, a Virgin company bought the first of two railways! With his wealth, he could have retired. But Richard Branson was having too much fun creating new businesses.

Chapter 7
Helping Others

As The Virgin Group grew, Richard Branson's smiling face was recognized around the world. He saw that his wealth and fame put him in a position to help others.

In 1987, Richard started a charity called the Healthcare Foundation. Its goal was to try to stop the spread of HIV and AIDS and to fight other health problems.

HIV/AIDS

DURING THE 1980S, A NEW VIRUS CALLED HIV BROKE OUT IN THE UNITED STATES. IT LED TO A DISEASE CALLED AIDS. DOCTORS NOW USE THE TERM HIV/AIDS TO REPRESENT A LARGE GROUP OF DISEASES CAUSED BY THE HIV VIRUS. THE HIV VIRUS WEAKENS A PERSON'S IMMUNE SYSTEM—THE BODY'S NATURAL DEFENSE AGAINST DISEASE. AN AIDS PATIENT IS MUCH MORE LIKELY TO GET INFECTIONS THAT CANNOT BE HEALED.

IN THE 1980S, WHEN RICHARD BECAME INTERESTED IN FIGHTING THE SPREAD OF HIV/AIDS, MOST PEOPLE INFECTED WITH THE VIRUS DIED. TODAY, THERE ARE A NUMBER OF MEDICATIONS THAT KEEP HIV/AIDS PATIENTS HEALTHY ENOUGH TO LIVE WITH THE DISEASE.

Richard also developed a strong interest in the nation of South Africa. The country was once led by a small group of white South Africans who denied black residents their legal rights. Finally, in 1994, black South Africans voted for the first time, and Nelson Mandela was elected the country's first black president. After Mandela became president, Virgin began doing business in South Africa. Richard also bought land there in 1999, which is now a private game reserve called Ulusaba. The wildlife there was protected

NELSON MANDELA

from hunters. Richard had a home at Ulusaba and loved watching giraffes and elephants roam the land. Today, visitors can stay at Ulusaba and enjoy the wildlife of South Africa.

BRANSON CENTRE OF ENTREPRENEURSHIP

Richard wanted to help South Africans become business owners. In 2005, the Healthcare Foundation, now renamed Virgin Unite, helped open a school there called the Branson Centre of Entrepreneurship. Entrepreneurs are people like Richard—they have an idea for a business they want to start and run on their own. Richard believed that creating entrepreneurs around the world would help poor countries become richer.

Richard knew that his planes and trains added to the problem of climate change and global warming. They ran on the fuels that created harmful gases. He also knew people couldn't stop traveling. So, he decided to do what he could to address the problem. In 2006, Richard started Virgin Fuels, to make cleaner "green" fuels, which are better for the environment than traditional fuel. The next year, Virgin Green Fund appeared. The Green Fund invests in small companies that make products that save energy or help the environment. And in 2007, Richard created the Virgin Earth Challenge. He would give $25 million to anyone

who found a way to remove harmful gases from the air in an effort to help slow climate change.

By 2000, Richard was one of the richest and most famous men in Great Britain. That year, Queen Elizabeth II knighted him for his skills as an entrepreneur. He could now be called Sir Richard Branson. Receiving the honor, he was thinking of the many Virgin Group employees. He said, "They have all worked very hard to make Virgin what it is, and I am accepting this honor on behalf of them."

THE WISDOM OF THE ELDERS

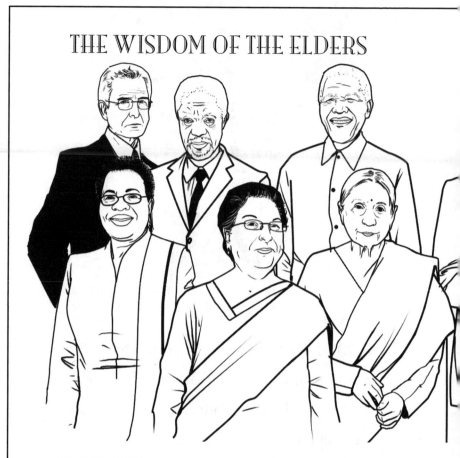

IN THE EARLY 2000S, RICHARD APPROACHED NELSON MANDELA WITH AN IDEA. RICHARD AND THE MUSICIAN PETER GABRIEL WANTED TO BRING TOGETHER RESPECTED WORLD LEADERS TO HELP END WARS AND PROMOTE EQUAL RIGHTS. MANDELA AGREED TO WORK WITH THEM, AND THEY FOUNDED THE ELDERS IN 2007. VIRGIN UNITE SPENT $18 MILLION TO SUPPORT THE ELDERS' EFFORTS.

FORMER US PRESIDENT JIMMY CARTER JOINED
THE GROUP. SO DID FORMER LEADERS FROM
MEXICO, BRAZIL, IRELAND, AND OTHER COUNTRIES.
THE ELDERS HAVE TRIED TO PROMOTE PEACE IN
AFRICA AND THE MIDDLE EAST. THEY HAVE ALSO
CALLED ON ALL NATIONS TO REDUCE THE CREATION
OF GASES THAT ARE WARMING THE PLANET.

Chapter 8
To Space—and Beyond

Richard hadn't taken his first airplane trip until he was in his twenties. But flying had quickly become a huge part of his life. He built one of his most successful companies around airplanes.

He won fame for his daring balloon flights. As his wealth grew, Richard looked even higher into the skies. He imagined a day when companies, not governments, would carry passengers into space. He already had a name for his own space-travel company: Virgin Galactic.

Richard talked to different inventors who were building new spacecraft. They hoped to be able to take passengers into the lowest levels of space, about sixty miles above Earth, and return the same day. One of these inventors was Burt Rutan. He designed two vehicles that could one day carry people into space.

BURT RUTAN

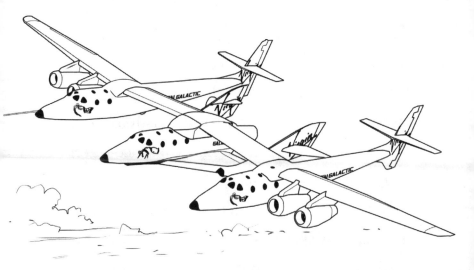

The first one was a large plane that carried a smaller aircraft underneath it. Passengers were to sit inside the smaller aircraft, along with one pilot.

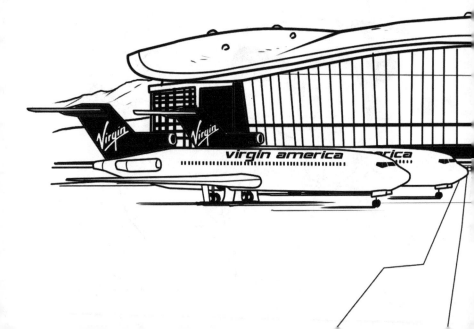

When the plane reached fifty thousand feet, it released the smaller aircraft, which soared fifty miles above Earth.

Rutan built and tested his first spacecraft in October 2004. Richard then gave Rutan the money to build an even better spacecraft. Virgin Galactic was open for business. Hundreds of people paid $250,000 to reserve a seat on future flights.

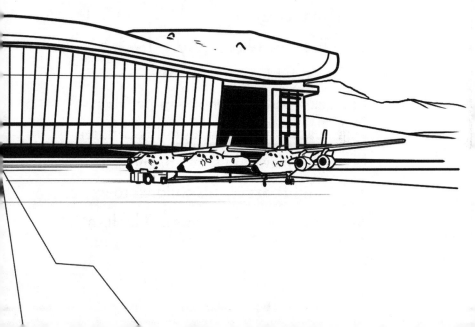

Richard was eager to become the first person to fly on Virgin Galactic. But getting into space would take years, as the company tested and retested the new designs of its spacecraft. In the meantime, Richard continued to work with his charities, to start new companies, and to expand existing ones.

Necker Island remained important to Richard and his family. He said it had become "a place where the whole family felt at home and at peace." Richard taught his children Sam and Holly to play tennis, swim, and sail there. Richard didn't expect his children to work in the family business. His parents had let him

choose his own path in life. But he welcomed
Holly and Sam when they became adults and
chose to join The Virgin Group on their own.

Given all the good times the Bransons shared at Necker, no one was surprised that Holly planned to have her wedding there in 2011. But before her marriage to Freddy Andrews, lightning sparked a fire in the Branson home. It quickly burned to the ground.

Several months later, the wedding went on in front of the burned wreckage, with Richard promising to build a new and even bigger home.

That same year, Richard showed that at sixty-one years old he still had an adventurous streak.

He had learned kite-surfing, a sport that combines sailing and surfing. Richard sailed across the English Channel, a distance of about twenty-two miles. He once again set a record, becoming the oldest person to make the channel crossing.

When he isn't traveling, Richard spends a lot of time at Necker Island. He enjoys writing blogs and posting on Twitter. He is passionate about sharing his ideas on how to become a successful entrepreneur. The different Virgin companies now have more than sixty thousand employees around the world. Richard's personal fortune has grown to nearly $5 billion. But to Richard, "Business is simply creating something that people want." All his life, Richard sought out new challenges. Almost always, he succeeded. He keeps looking for them and has plenty of fun along the way.

THE GIVING PLEDGE

WHILE MANY PEOPLE ADMIRE RICHARD BRANSON'S BUSINESS SUCCESS, HIS OWN HERO IS ANOTHER ENTREPRENEUR—BILL GATES. GATES BECAME THE RICHEST PERSON IN THE WORLD AFTER CREATING THE SOFTWARE COMPANY MICROSOFT. IN 2000, GATES BEGAN GIVING AWAY BILLIONS OF DOLLARS TO FIGHT HUNGER AND DISEASES AROUND THE WORLD.

BILL GATES

IN 2010, GATES—ALONG WITH HIS FRIEND WARREN BUFFETT—STARTED THE GIVING PLEDGE.

AS BILLIONAIRES, THE TWO MEN PLEDGED TO
SHARE THEIR WEALTH WITH OTHERS. THEY WANTED
OTHER BILLIONAIRES TO PROMISE TO GIVE AWAY
MOST OF THEIR MONEY TO CHARITY.

IN 2013, RICHARD JOINED THE GIVING PLEDGE.
HE SAID, "STUFF REALLY IS NOT WHAT BRINGS
HAPPINESS. FAMILY, FRIENDS, GOOD HEALTH, AND
THE SATISFACTION THAT COMES FROM MAKING
A POSITIVE DIFFERENCE ARE WHAT REALLY
MATTERS." RICHARD WOULD PREFER THAT HIS
MONEY GO TO PEOPLE IN NEED OR TO THOSE
WHO ARE TRYING TO IMPROVE THE WORLD.

TIMELINE OF
RICHARD BRANSON'S LIFE

1950	Born on July 18, 1950, in London, England
1967	Moves to London to start *Student* magazine and publishes the first issue the next year
1970	Starts Virgin Mail Order to sell records
1972	Marries Kristen Tomassi
1973	Launches Virgin Records and has a huge hit with Mike Oldfield's *Tubular Bells*
1976	Divorces Kristen and meets Joan Templeman
1978	Buys Necker Island
1981	Daughter Holly is born
1984	Starts Virgin Atlantic Airways
1985	Son Sam is born
1986	Sets a speed record crossing the Atlantic Ocean by boat
1987	Becomes the first person to cross the Atlantic in a hot-air balloon. Starts the Healthcare Foundation to fight HIV and AIDS
1989	Marries Joan at Necker Island
1992	Sells Virgin Records and becomes a billionaire
2000	Is knighted by Queen Elizabeth II
2004	Opens Virgin Galactic to bring people into space
2007	Founds the Elders with Nelson Mandela and Peter Gabriel. Virgin America begins flying in the United States
2011	Sets a record as the oldest man to kite-surf across the English Channel
2013	Takes the Giving Pledge and promises to give most of his wealth to charity

TIMELINE OF
THE WORLD

Elizabeth II becomes Queen of England	1952
Sputnik I is launched into space	1957
The Beatles have their first number-one song in England	1963
US ground troops arrive to fight in Vietnam	1965
Students across Europe and the United States protest the Vietnam War	1968
Apollo 11 lands the first humans on the moon	1969
Richard Nixon resigns as president of the United States	1974
Bill Gates and Paul Allen found Microsoft	1975
Margaret Thatcher is the first woman elected prime minister of Great Britain	1979
Great Britain defeats Argentina in war to control the Falkland Islands Michael Jackson releases *Thriller*, which becomes the best-selling album of all time	1982
The World Wide Web is launched	1991
South Africa has its first free elections	1994
Terrorists launch several attacks in the United States, killing almost three thousand people	2001
Spaceport America, the future home of Virgin Galactic, launches its first commercial flight outside Truth or Consequences, New Mexico	2006
Barack Obama is elected the first African American president of the United States	2008
Nelson Mandela dies	2013

BIBLIOGRAPHY

Bowker, Tom. **Branson**. London: HarperPerennial, 2008.

Branson, Eve. **Mum's the Word: The High-Flying Adventures of Eve Branson**. Milton Keynes, England: AuthorHouseUK, 2013.

Branson, Richard. **Losing My Virginity: How I Survived, Had Fun, and Made a Fortune Doing Business My Way**. New York: Crown Business, 2007.

Branson, Richard. **Reach for the Skies: Ballooning, Birdmen & Blasting Into Space**. London: Virgin Books, 2010.

Brown, Mick. **Richard Branson: The Inside Story**. London: Headline, 1989.

* Books for young readers

* Burgan, Michael. **Popular Culture: 1960–1979**. Chicago: Heinemann Raintree, 2013.

Cadzow, Jame. "Outer Reaches." **Sydney Morning Herald**, June 15, 2013. Online at http://www.smh.com.au/technology/sci-tech/outer-reaches-20130614-2nyxd.html

* Demuth, Patricia Brennan. **Who Is Bill Gates?** New York: Grosset & Dunlap, 2013.

* Gogerly, Liz. **Richard Branson: Daredevil Entrepreneur**. London: Wayland, 2010.

Vinnedge, Mary. "Richard Branson: Virgin Entrepreneur." **SUCCESS magazine**. 2009. Online at http://www.success.com/article/richard-branson-virgin-entrepreneur